I enjoyed art, and thought I could achieve a good grade in this subject, but English was not my strongest subject; spelling was definitely a weak point.

On the very day I left school, I started the long walk back home. I had no money to pay for the bus, therefore, I had no choice but to walk or hitch a lift home. No sooner had I stuck out my thumb for a lift, a car pulled up and the driver announced he was passing through my village. In conversation, the driver mentioned that he was new to the area and was looking for an apprentice to train as a sign writer. I promptly replied 'I'm available and can start in the morning.' The driver introduced himself to my parents, explained what the job involved and arranged to pick me up the following morning.

That was over thirty years ago and I still can't spell.

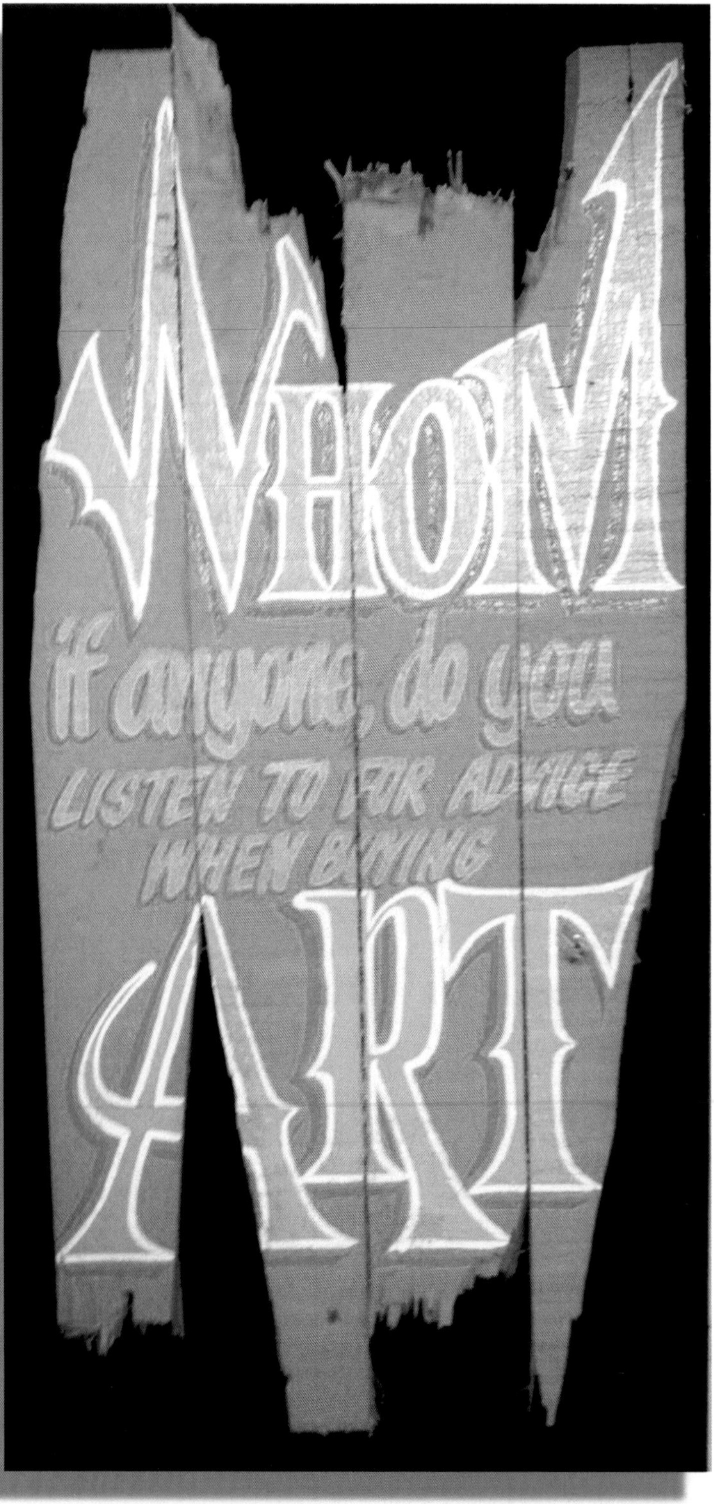
WHOM
if anyone, do you
LISTEN TO FOR ADVICE
WHEN BUYING
ART

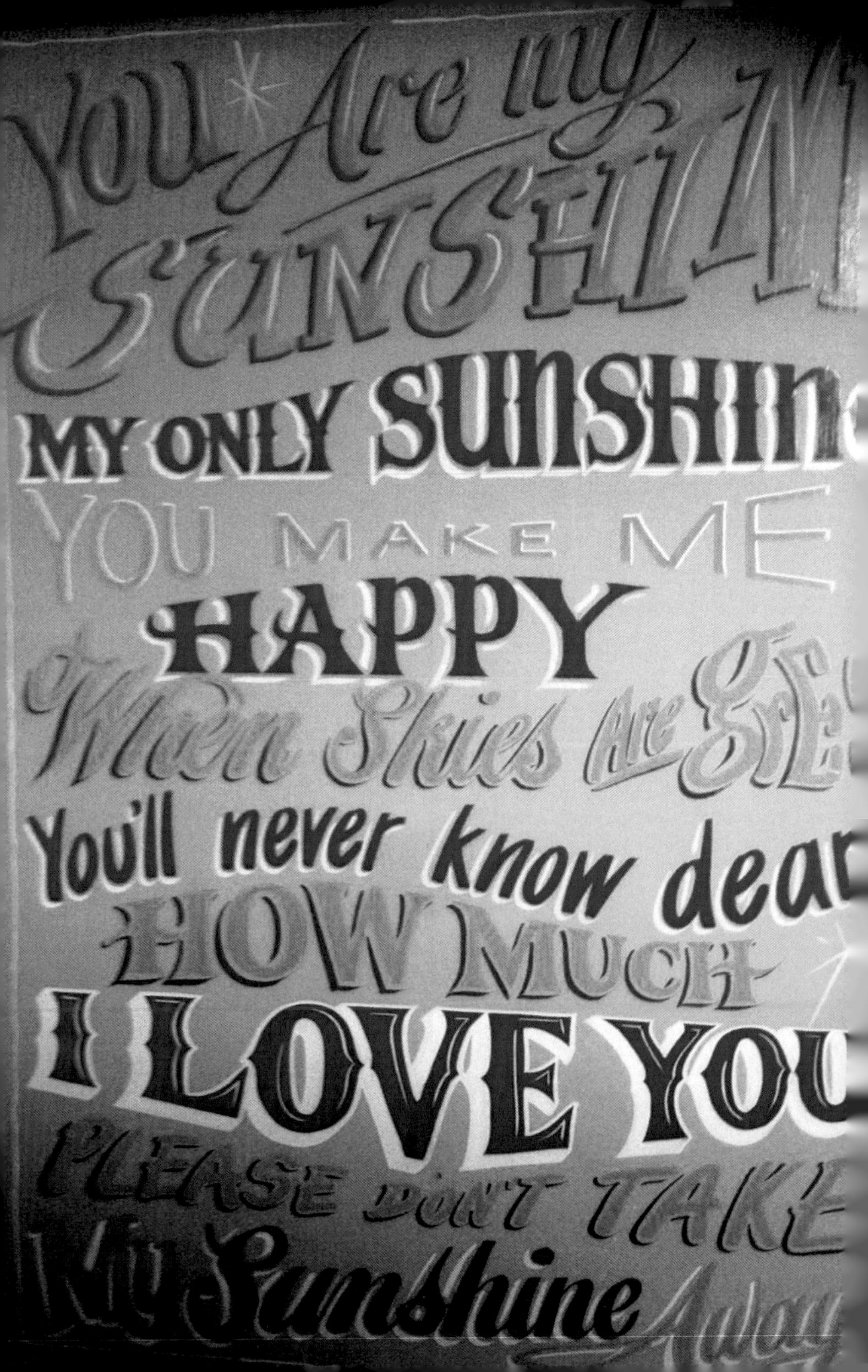

You Are my
SUNSHIN
MY ONLY SUNSHIN
YOU MAKE ME
HAPPY
When Skies Are Gre
You'll never know dea
HOW MUCH
I LOVE YOU
PLEASE DON'T TAKE
Sunshine

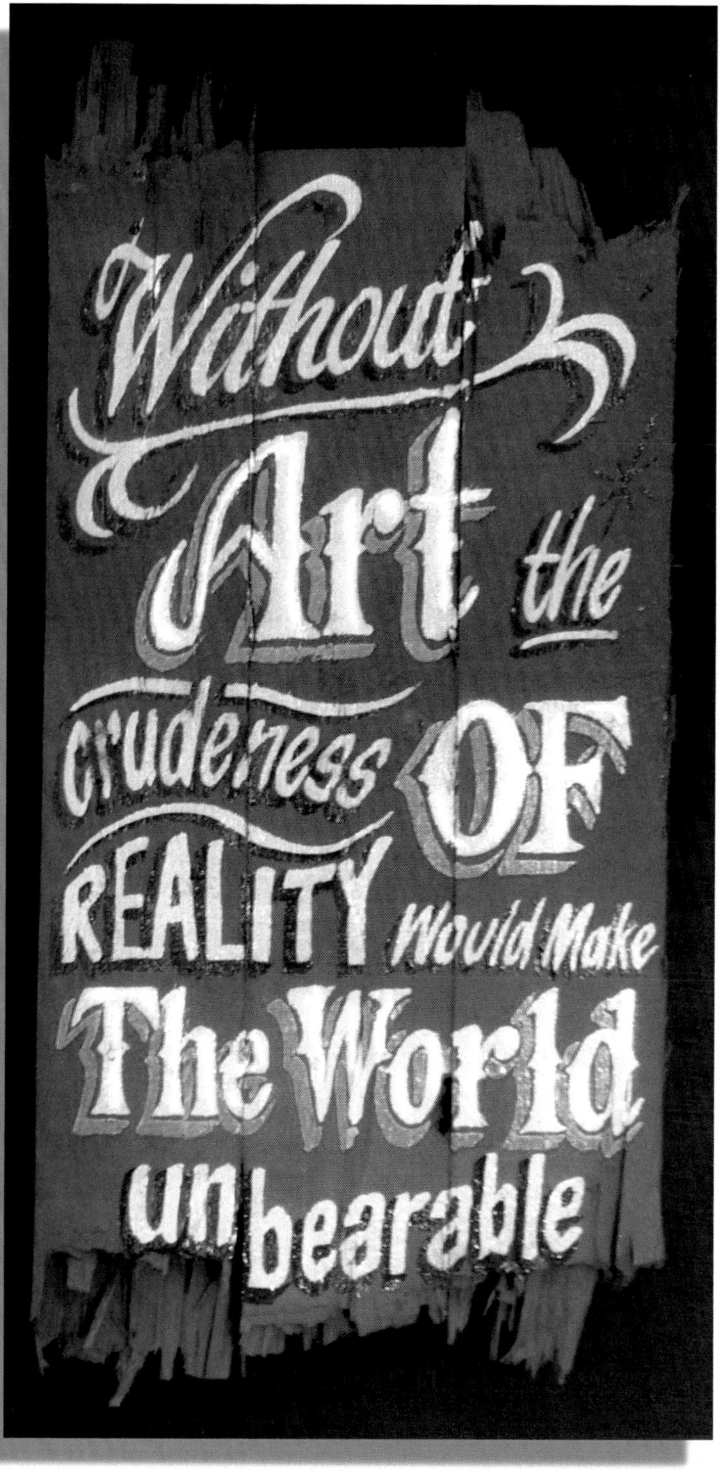
Without
Art the
crudeness OF
REALITY Would Make
The World
unbearable

AvyO UEvE

rgAZe

dATapA

InTIng&

aNdTH

OuGH

ttHAT

scRAP

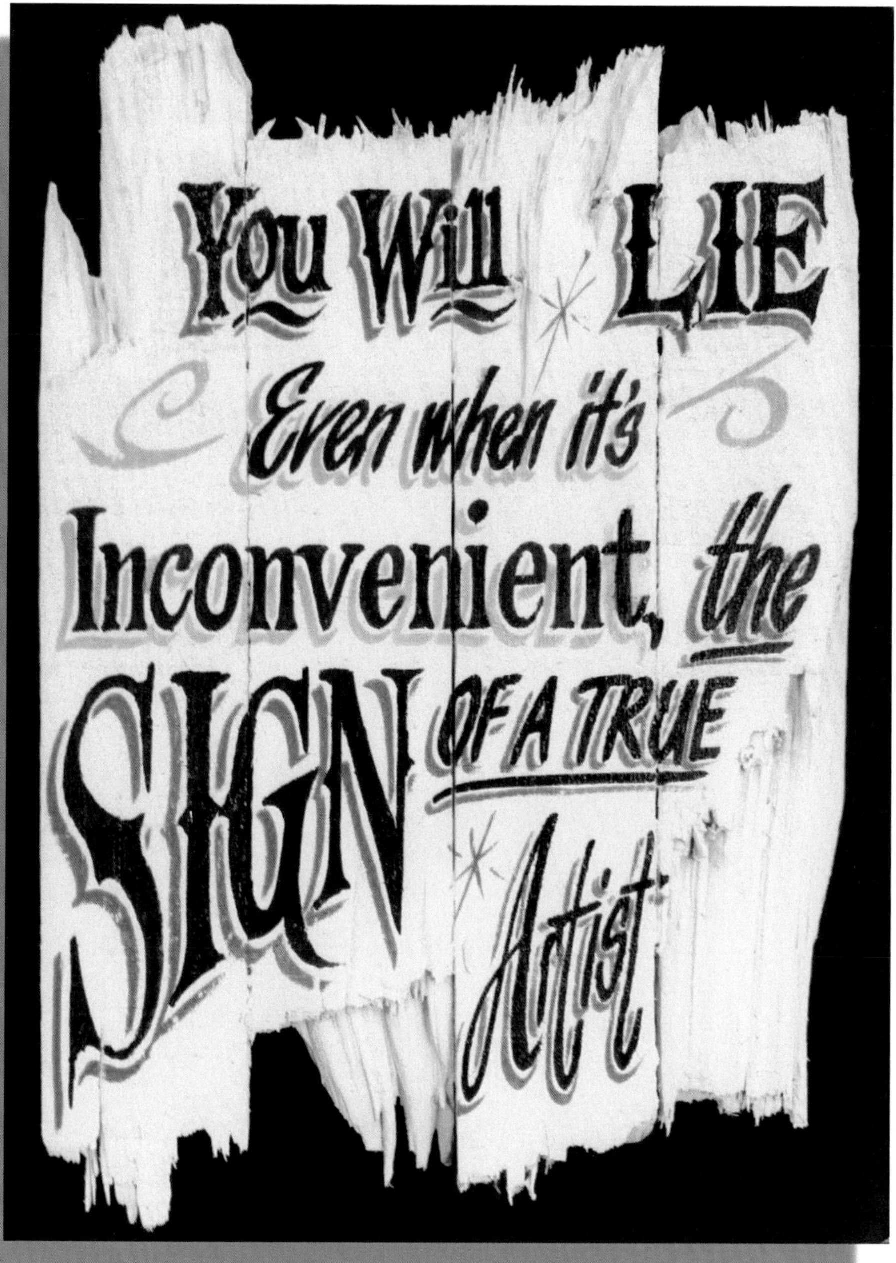
You Will LIE
Even when it's
Inconvenient, the
SIGN OF A TRUE
Artist

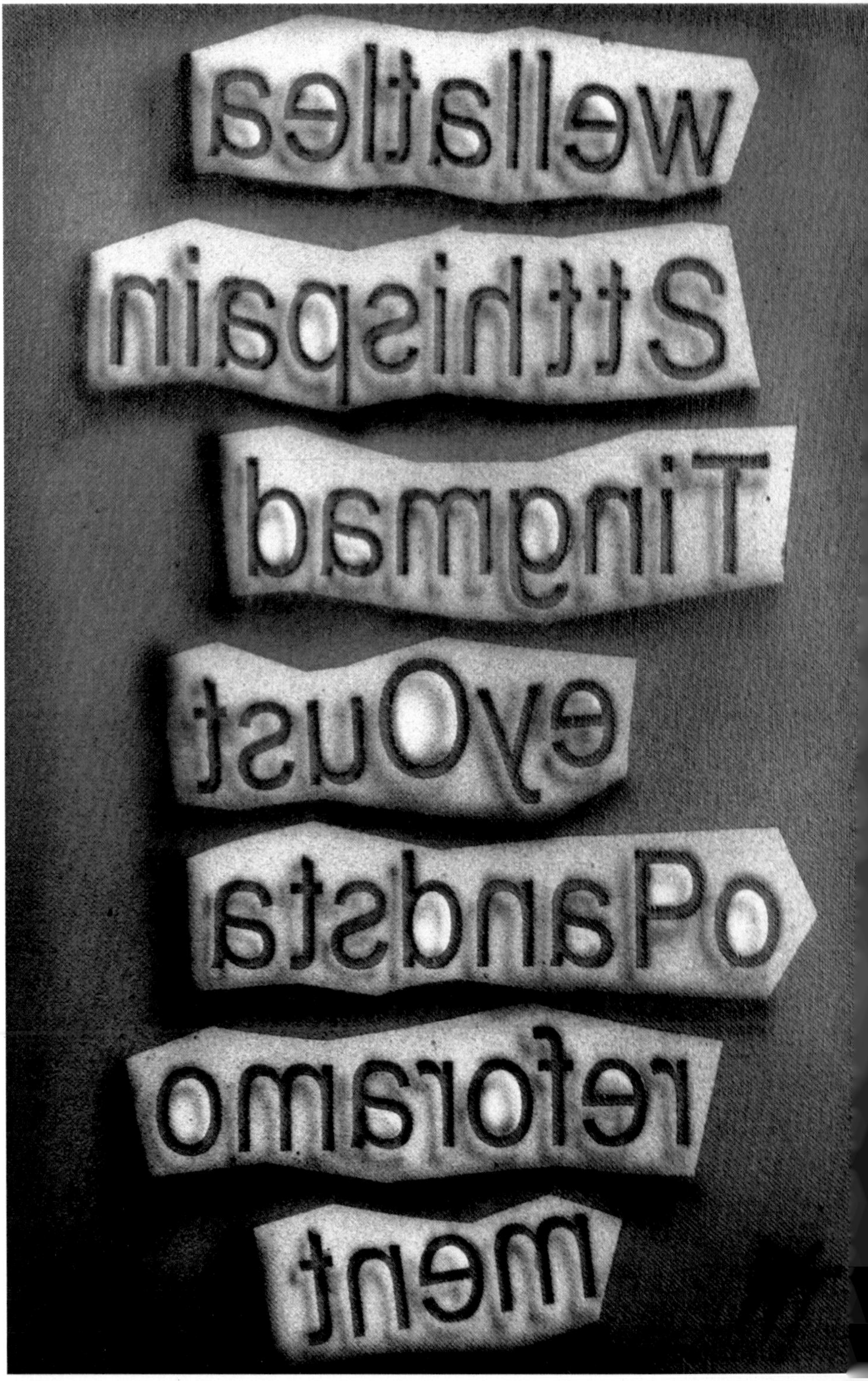

wellatlea

atthispain

Tingmad

eYOust

oQandsta

reforamo

ment

Are Art CRITICS all failed Artists, and Dismissed AS SUCH? OR is there no such thing AS A FAILED Artist

it's not
hard to understand
Modern ART
If it hangs on a wall
it's a painting

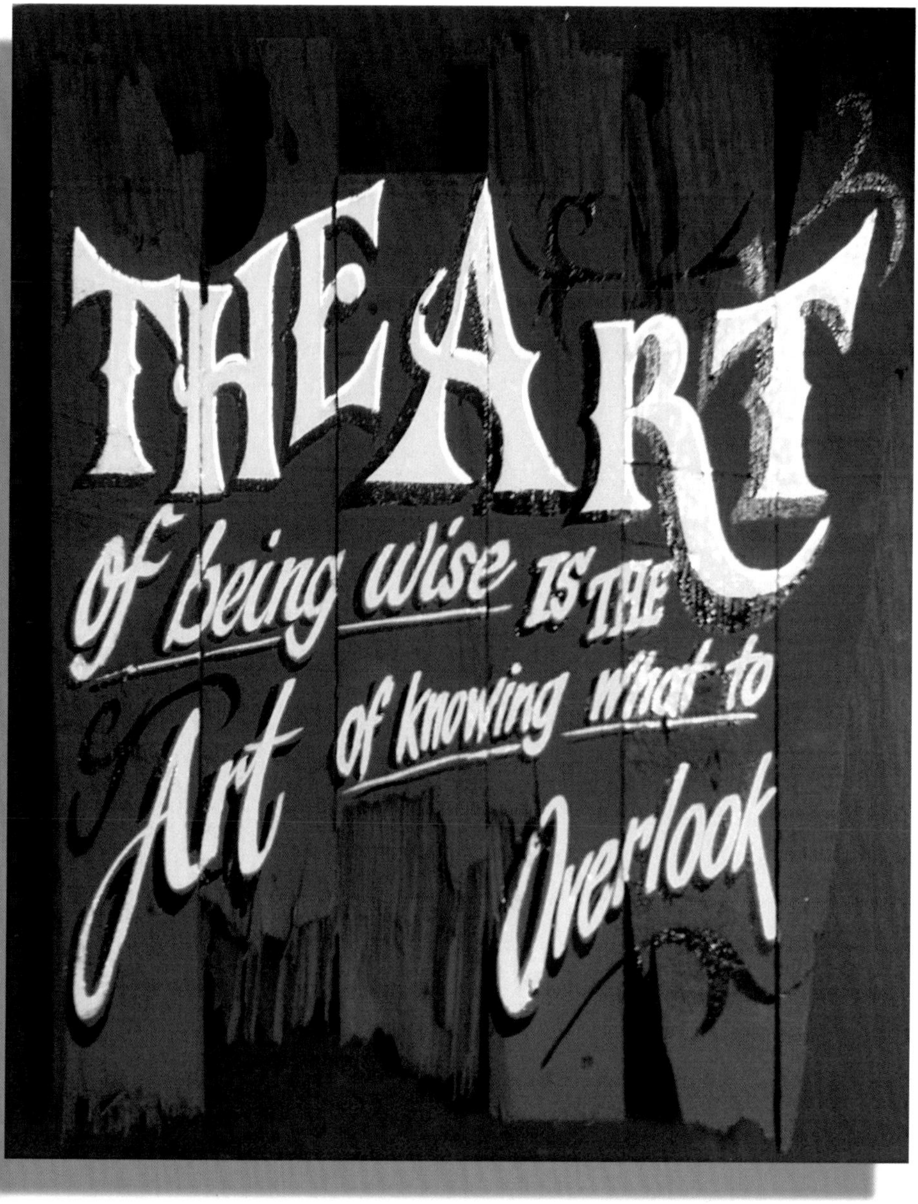
THE ART
of being wise IS THE
Art of knowing what to
Overlook

The Signs They Are A-Changin'

The More You Like ART, the More ART you Like. So Buy Lots Of It, SEEING Art AS AN investment would take away All the FUN

I have been signwriting for over thirty years and I still love the feel of a sable brush, the texture of enamel paint and of course the interesting and sometimes challenging commissions.

The most common question I get asked when people see me working is,

`Isn't that a dying art`

Some of the images in this book show where traditional signwriting is still used.

Traditional sign writing has been considered

'A dying art.' The main reason for this is the widespread use of computer aided sign plotters that produce Plastic vinyl stickers. The effect of modern technology meant that many traditional sign writers now use computers to do the work.

As a traditionalist, I continue to use the original hand and brush technique.

Using iPads and PC's, clients often design their own signs and expect a sign writer to paint absolutely any font chosen from their computer. Computers have several variations of most fonts, such as 'script'. There is 'Palace, English and Brush script.' I then have to explain to customers that unless they want me to trace the letters individually, which is time consuming and will look like a computer image, there is no point in having it hand painted.

Every sign writer paints differently, even if we all have the same information, we are not machines programed for perfection. When commissioned to paint a sign and the font requirements are Script, Old English or Roman, we paint our interpretation that is both unique and aesthetically pleasing. Slight imperfections must be tolerated, such as feathered edges and brush marks. These slight imperfections add character and authenticity to hand painted signs.

Before plywood became popular at the time of the Second World War, signs were painted directly onto brickwork and masonry. Today, most of the large

commercial signs are plastic. There are some buildings in conservation areas that still require traditional hand painted signs. You can still see faded letters on some old buildings; these images are known as 'Ghost Signs.' Most of these signs were set out by using a paper template and pounce wheel. A pounce wheel is a sharp spiked wheel that you roll around the contours of a design, creating a perforated outline. A pounce pad loaded with powder is then tapped over the design leaving a fine line of chalk dots giving you a guideline to paint to.

Writing Wrongs

I'm someone who relies on a dictionary daily but this does not mean I'm exempt from making mistakes. In fact, I have made several over the last thirty years, and I'm not ashamed to admit this. I'm not a walking dictionary and little distractions whilst writing can result in silly errors being made even when writing the simplest word.

I was once commissioned to paint a 'Fancy dress party' sign for a Hotel, for the New Year's Eve party. The Hotel was situated in the middle of a beautiful village and the sign was 6ft high, so everybody could read it.

Whilst painting the sign, I stopped to answer my phone. On completion, the hotelier stood back and admired his new sign before paying me.

About ten days later, I received a phone call **'You've spelt it wrong!'** Of course I rushed back to the hotel to correct it, but by this time several people had spotted the mistake and word had spread around the village. The Hotelier thanked me for making such a mistake because this had become the talking point of the village giving his party wider publicity. The sign read **'Fanny dress party.'** And one passing tourist laughed and said 'so that's what you get up to in the country!'

AnyoNewh
ohaseverst
ruggleDwi
thpovertyk
nowsHOw
extreMELyE
xpenSiveit
iStobepoor

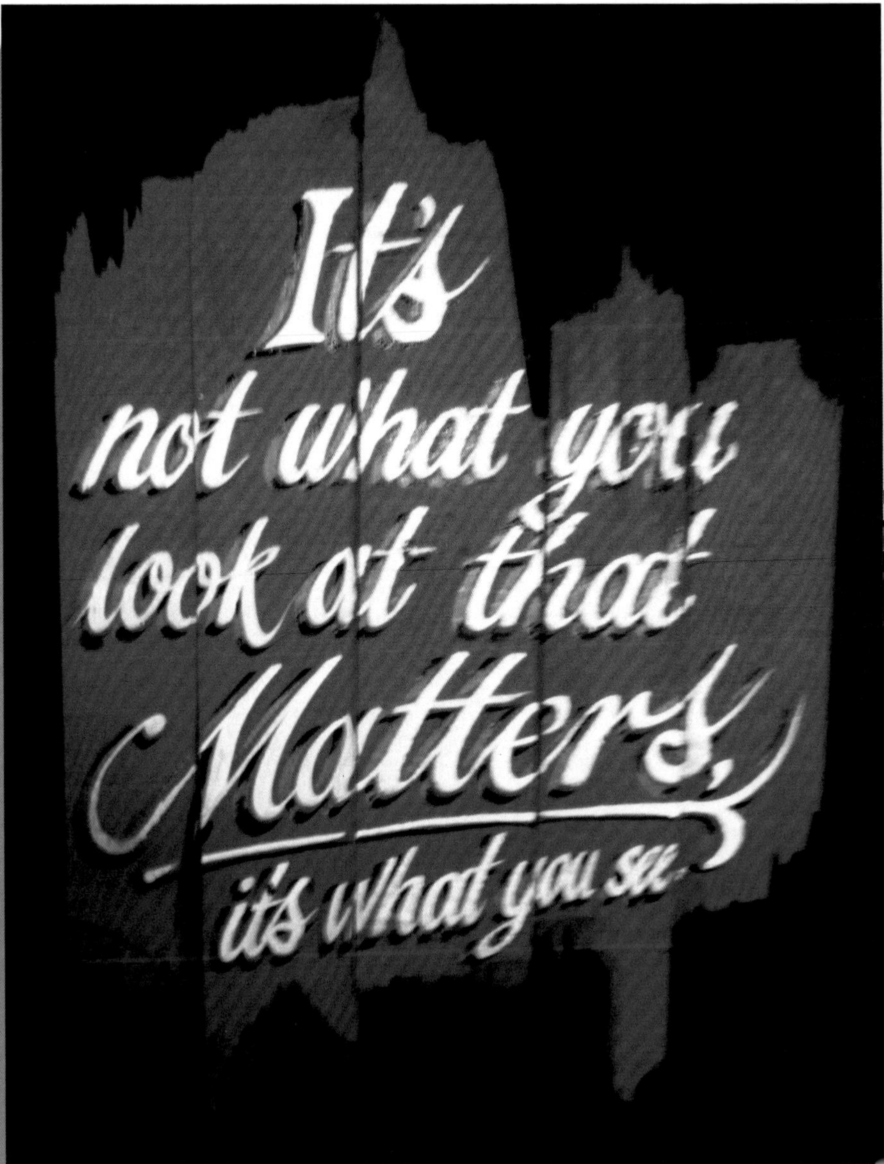
It's
not what you
look at that
Matters,
it's what you see.

The Art of Government

consists of taking As

MUCH MONEY

as possible FROM 1 Group

OF PEOPLE AND

GIVING it 2 Another...

Waterberry Zambezi Lodge

ZAMBIA

In February 2012 I had the pleasure of travelling to Africa to hand
paint about 80 signs for Waterberry Lodge in Zambia. During the
last 30 years, I have worked all over the United Kingdom includin
Scotland, Wales, Isle of Wight, London and the Home Counties,
but this was the most exciting trip of all. I feel honoured and
fortunate to work in such a beautiful country and have fond
memories of the people who made me most welcome.

TANSWELL PUBLICATIONS

LEARN HOW TO PAINT SIGNS, Introductory Guide

ISBN No: 978-0-9562463-0-1

LEARN HOW TO PAINT SIGNS, Freestyle Guide

ISBN No: 987-0-95624631-8

www.signwritingcourses.co.uk